WINTER NUMBERS

WINTER NUMBERS

POEMS

Marilyn Hacker

W · W · NORTON & COMPANY

NEW YORK · LONDON

FIRST EDITION

"Against Elegies" was first published in *The American Voice.*
"Nearly a Valediction" and "A Note Downriver" were first published in the *New Virginia Review.*
"Nearly a Valediction" also appeared in *MS;* it was included in the anthologies *No More Masks,* Florence Howe, Ed., HarperPerennial, 1993, and *An Intimate Wilderness: Lesbian Writers on Sexuality,* Judith Barrington, Ed., Eighth Mountain Press, 1991.
"Corona" was first published in the *Massachusetts Review.* It also appeared in the *Bread Loaf Anthology,* Sydney Lea, Ed.
"Groves of Academe" was published in *Open Places.*
"Days of 1987" was first published in the *Yale Review.*
"Elysian Fields," "Cleis," "Dusk: July," "Street Scenes II," "For a Fiftieth Anniversary," and "Year's End" were first published in the *Paris Review,* which also published "Cancer Winter."
"Year's End," with the title "Late November," also appeared in *MS.*
"Dusk: July" was also included in *A Formal Feeling,* Annie Finch, Ed., Milkweed Editions, 1994.
"Elysian Fields" was included in *Best American Poetry 1992,* Charles Simic, Ed., Collier Books, 1992.
"Cleis" and "Street Scenes II" also appeared in *Aquarius* (UK).
"One More Car Poem for Julie" was first published in *Puerto del Sol.*
"Annunciation: 8 A.M.," "Letter to Julie in a New Decade" and "An Absent Friend" were first published in *Boulevard.*
"Letter to Julie in a New Decade" and "An Absent Friend" also appeared in *Poetry Review* (UK).
"Her Ring," "Letter on June 15" and "Quai Saint-Bernard" were first published in the *Kenyon Review.*
"Letter to a Wound" was first published in *Ploughshares.*
"For K. J., Between Anniversaries" and "Chiliastic Sapphics" were first published in the *New England Review.*
"Days of 1992" was published by the *Colorado Review.*
"August Journal" was published in *Prairie Schooner.*
"Street Scenes I, III, IV & V" were published in *TriQuarterly.*
"Cancer Winter" received the John Masefield Memorial Award of the Poetry Society of America in 1994, and the B. F. Conners Award of the *Paris Review,* also in 1994.

Library of Congress Cataloging-in-Publication Data

Hacker, Marilyn, 1942–
    Winter numbers: poems / Marilyn Hacker.
       p.   cm.
    I. Title.
    PS3558.A28W56   1994
    811'.54—dc20   94-18615

ISBN 0-393-03674-X

W. W. Norton & Company, Inc., 500 Fifth Avenue, New York, N.Y. 10110
W. W. Norton & Company Ltd., 10 Coptic Street, London WC1A 1PU

1 2 3 4 5 6 7 8 9 0

FOR MARIE PONSOT

CONTENTS

AGAINST ELEGIES

ELYSIAN FIELDS

CANCER WINTER

Against Elegies

Against Elegies

for Catherine Arthur and Melvin Dixon

James has cancer. Catherine has cancer.
Melvin has AIDS.
Whom will I call, and get no answer?
My old friends, my new friends who are old,
or older, sixty, seventy, take pills
with meals or after dinner. Arthritis
scourges them. But irremediable night is
farther away from them; they seem to hold
it at bay better than the young-middle-aged
whom something, or another something, kills
before the chapter's finished, the play staged.
The curtains stay down when the light fades.

Morose, unanswerable, the list
of thirty- and forty-year-old suicides
(friends' lovers, friends' daughters) insists
in its lengthening: something's wrong.
The sixty-five-year-olds are splendid, vying
with each other in work hours and wit.
They bring their generosity along,
setting the tone, or not giving a shit.
How well, or how eccentrically, they dress!
Their anecdotes are to the point, or wide
enough to make room for discrepancies.
But their children are dying.

Natalie died by gas in Montpeyroux.
In San Francisco, Ralph died
of lung cancer, AIDS years later, Lew

wrote to me. Lew, who, at forty-five,
expected to be dead of drink, who, ten
years on, wasn't, instead, survived
a gentle, bright, impatient younger man.
(Cliché: he falls in love with younger men.)
Natalie's father came, and Natalie,
as if she never had been there, was gone.
Michèle closed up their house (where she
was born). She shrouded every glass inside

—mirrors, photographs—with sheets, as Jews
do, though she's not a Jew.
James knows, he thinks, as much as he wants to.
He hasn't seen a doctor since November.
They made the diagnosis in July.
Catherine is back in radiotherapy.
Her schoolboy haircut, prematurely gray,
now frames a face aging with other numbers:
"stage two," "stage three" mean more than "fifty-one"
and mean, precisely, nothing, which is why
she stares at nothing: lawn chair, stone,
bird, leaf; brusquely turns off the news.

I hope they will be sixty in ten years
and know I used their names
as flares in a polluted atmosphere,
as private reasons where reason obtains
no quarter. Children in the streets
still die in grandfathers' good wars.
Pregnant women with AIDS, schoolgirls, crack whores,
die faster than men do, in more pain,
are more likely than men to die alone.
And our statistics, on the day I meet

the lump in my breast, you phone
the doctor to see if your test results came?

The earth-black woman in the bed beside
Lidia on the AIDS floor—deaf, and blind:
I want to know if, no, how, she died.
The husband, who'd stopped visiting, returned?
He brought the little boy, those nursery-
school smiles taped on the walls? She traced
her name on Lidia's face
when one of them needed something. She learned
some Braille that week. Most of the time, she slept.
Nobody knew the baby's HIV
status. Sleeping, awake, she wept.
And I left her name behind.

And Lidia, where's she
who got her act so clean
of rum and Salem Filters and cocaine
after her passing husband passed it on?
As soon as she knew
she phoned and told her mother she had AIDS
but no, she wouldn't come back to San Juan.
Sipping *café con leche* with dessert,
in a blue robe, thick hair in braids,
she beamed: her life was on the right
track, now. But the cysts hurt
too much to sleep through the night.

No one was promised a shapely life
ending in a tutelary vision.
No one was promised: if
you're a genuinely irreplaceable

grandmother or editor
you will not need to be replaced.
When I die, the death I face
will more than likely be illogical:
Alzheimer's or a milk truck: the absurd.
The Talmud teaches we become impure
when we die, profane dirt, once the word
that spoke this life in us has been withdrawn,

the letter taken from the envelope.
If we believe the letter will be read,
some curiosity, some hope
come with knowing that we die.
But this was another century
in which we made death humanly obscene:
Soweto El Salvador Kurdistan
Armenia Shatila Baghdad Hanoi
Auschwitz   Each one, unique as our lives are,
taints what's left with complicity,
makes everyone living a survivor
who will, or won't bear witness for the dead.

I can only bear witness for my own
dead and dying, whom I've often failed:
unanswered letters, unattempted phone
calls, against these fictions. A fiction winds
her watch in sunlight, cancer ticking bone
to shards. A fiction looks
at proofs of a too-hastily finished book
that may be published before he goes blind.
The old, who tell good stories, half expect
that what's written in their chromosomes
will come true, that history won't interject
a virus or a siren or a sealed

train to where age is irrelevant.
The old rebbetzin at Ravensbrück
died in the most wrong place, at the wrong time.
What do the young know different?
No partisans are waiting in the woods
to welcome them. Siblings who stayed home
count down doom. Revolution became
a dinner party in a fast-food chain,
a vendetta for an abscessed crime,
a hard-on market for consumer goods.
A living man reads a dead woman's book.
She wrote it; then, he knows, she was turned in.

For every partisan
there are a million gratuitous
deaths from hunger, all-American
mass murders, small wars,
the old diseases and the new.
Who dies well? The privilege
of asking doesn't have to do with age.
For most of us
no question what our deaths, our lives, mean.
At the end, Catherine will know what she knew,
and James will, and Melvin,
and I, in no one's stories, as we are.

ELYSIAN FIELDS

Nearly a Valediction

You happened to me. I was happened to
like an abandoned building by a bull-
dozer, like the van that missed my skull
happened a two-inch gash across my chin.
You went as deep down as I'd ever been.
You were inside me like my pulse. A new-
born flailing toward maternal heartbeat through
the shock of cold and glare: when you were gone,
swaddled in strange air, I was that alone
again, inventing life left after you.

I don't want to remember you as that
four-o'clock-in-the-morning eight months long
after you happened to me like a wrong
number at midnight that blew up the phone
bill to an astronomical unknown
quantity in foreign currency.
The dollar's dived since you happened to me.
You've grown into your skin since then; you've grown
into the space you measure with someone
you can love back without a caveat.

While I love somebody I learn to live
with through the downpulled winter days' routine
wakings and sleepings, half-and-half caffeine-
assisted mornings, laundry, stockpots, dust
balls in the hallway, lists instead of lust
sometimes, instead of longing, trust
that what comes next comes after what came first.
She'll never be a story I make up.

You were the one I didn't know where to stop.
If I had blamed you, now I could forgive

you, but what made my cold hand, back in prox-
imity to your hair, your mouth, your mind,
want where it no way ought to be, defined
by where it was, and was and was until
the whole globed swelling liquefied and spilled
through one cheek's nap, a syllable, a tear,
wasn't blame, whatever I wished it were.
You were the weather in my neighborhood.
You were the epic in the episode.
You were the year poised on the equinox.

Terminal

When what you want turns into what you need
you run the risk of running into debt:
the lease comes up and will not be renewed.

It was too good to last, the nest, the *pied
à terre* where I had landed, and I let
what I wanted turn into what I need.

The priest-landlord was in a venal mood:
"Mitigeur de la baignoire qui éclate!
The lease comes up, and will not be renewed!"

—transforming my contentment into greed
to hold what I once had. You're desperate
when what you want turns into what you need.

For sale now at a price I can't afford:
some Belgian adman gets a weekend flat.
The lease comes up and will not be renewed.

My best offer translates to a subdued
valediction to a habitat.
When what you want turns into what you need,
the lease comes up, and will not be renewed.

A Note Downriver

Afternoon of hungover Sunday morning
earned by drinking wine on an empty stomach
after I met Tom for a bomb on Broadway:
done worse; known better.

I feel muggy-headed and convalescent,
barely push a pen across blue-lined paper,
scowl at envelopes with another country's
stamps, and your letter.

Hilltop house, a river to take you somewhere,
sandwiches at noon with a good companion:
summer's ghost flicked ash from the front porch railing,
looked up, and listened.

I would grouse and growl at you if you called me.
I have made you chamomile tea and rye bread
toast, fixed us both orange juice laced with seltzer
similar mornings.

We'll most likely live in each other's houses
like I haunted yours last July, as long as
we hear rivers vacillate downstream. They say
"always"; say "never."

Corona

for Kim Vaeth

You're flying back, weighted with half the books
that piled the work table and the night table.
They bulk your rucksack. You gum on a label,
consign it, while our eyes condense three weeks
talk, silence, touch: relief, regret. It looks
like complicity. Friends, with a third friend,
I put my hand on your nape; you put your hand
in my back pocket. I kiss, first, both cheeks,
surprise you on your mouth. Your flight's called. I
watch you, helmed with departure, stubborn, brave
in cream shirt, lilac trousers, suede shoes, tie
the next tan, turn, glisten, go. Concave
space takes you, the cord's cut. We leave. I crave
uncomplicated quiet, and the sky.

Uncomplicated quiet, and the sky
a Marian mantle through the car window.
I think of all the things I'll never know.
"I wish I was older," the young girl said. "Why?"
"So I would know more." You and she and I
spanned twenty years among us. While you drove
serpent curves through vineyards and olive groves,
she read *The Bell Jar*, till we stopped to buy
Chianti at a *cave*, upturned the bell
to shining tulips where the garnet wine
perfumed our morning. Weight in the palm, see, smell,
taste: our three mouths contemplated fine
meditations of ancient earth, as well
considered as just measures for a line.

Considered as just measures for a line,
sound more than sense determines words I choose,
invention mutes intention. If the shoes
you bought were gray suede clogs, size thirty-nine,
if we sang passion's matins and compline,
I'm storytelling. Reading poetry
we expect truth, you said, and I agree.
Truth, in particulars, I can define.
They're brown, your oxfords, and size forty-one;
two nuns, watching over another nun
through a night of fever, could not have kept
their limbs more ordered than we did; we slept
apart, together: facile franchise, whose
unsubtle truth can blanket subtlety.

Unsubtle truth can blanket subtlety.
In the next room, you slept in our guest-friend bed.
Where I wrote, your pad sat, pen-marked. I read
that morning, what, that night, you'd thought of me.
I wished I could evaporate, could be
anywhere else. I thought "Ingratitude,"
and flinched, while Tuscan light ignored my mood.
If I fail friendship, what felicity
left? Words crystallize despite our lives, select
emblems from hesitations and suspect
feelings. I coaxed your questioning, oblique,
till words undid what they had done. We speak
our pieces: peace. Plural, and amical,
we crossed the Arno, walked beyond the wall.

We cross the Arno, walk beyond the wall
up a steep wooded hill I climbed before
with another woman, hand in hand.
Now we hold hands, too, meaning something more

and less than "sex." At the ramparts, we stand
looking down sungilt waves of clay roof tile
tender in late light slanted, now, toward Fall.
We separate ourselves from day-trip style
tourists, though we are tourists after all.
We need a breather from the personal.
Facts permit us touch. You rest your head on
my lap while I praise Suzanne Valadon.
Fatigue relaxes to repose in your
tanned shoulders, opulent and muscular.

Tanned shoulders, opulent and muscular,
power exuberant strokes. The choppy lake
frames, then conceals, your dolphin play. You take
a deep breath and submerge, then surface, far
away, all shining. There's a rectangular
concrete slab on pillars we saw boys make
lolloping dives from. You swim to it, break
thigh-high from the water, stretch to it, are
pendant by your wet arms, straining to pull
yourself up by them, drop, splash, leap again
determined from the water, less playful
now, challenged. You fall back. After ten
tries, you heave your leg over, stand, know I've
watched. I photograph your offhand dive.

Watched, I photograph your offhand dive.
How to depict attention that surveys
ground for reflexive confidence. Delays
are legion. When I navigate, you drive
home that indecision makes you arrive
exhausted anywhere. The hand belays
the rope to you's not mine. After a day's
mileage, Motown, nineteen-sixty-five;

we sing the car the last dark miles: "You can't
hurry love." We're almost what's almost home
to me. The constellated coast invokes
those road blues I'll sing myself, revenant
on airport buses when, again alone,
I'm flying back, weighted with half the books.

Groves of Academe

The hour dragged on, and I was badly needing
coffee; that encouraged my perversity.
I asked the students of Poetry Writing,
"Tell me about the poetry you're reading."
There was some hair chewing and some nail biting.
Snowdrifts piled up around the university.
"I've really gotten into science fiction."
"I don't read much—it breaks my concentration.
I wouldn't want to influence my style."
"We taped some Sound Poems for the college station."
"When *I* give readings, should I work on diction?"
"Is it true that no really worthwhile
contemporary poets write in rhyme?"
"Do you think it would be a waste of time
to send my poems to *Vanity Fair*?
I mean—could they relate to my work there?"

Days of 1987

We were coming down from the monastery
when a huge gray monk on a squat brown donkey,
cowled and bearded, brandished a furled umbrella
to flag our Vespa.

"Storm!" in Greek, I got from his words and gesture
(not a malediction on noon intruders).
Thunderheads piled up on the dark Aegean
cliffs, with no shelter

in the hills we'd wanted to wander over
after lunch, with oranges in your knapsack
saved for when we'd peeled back the afternoon to
nakedness, later.

Down around the sheepshit and potholes, sudden
gravel craters macadam never leveled,
arms around your cornflower shirt, I gripped you:
we both were freezing.

One hill village farther, the road got better.
Yellow roses flapped in the wind like dishrags
on the stucco wall of a house I wished were
ours for the season.

The archaic patriarch sky behind us
threatened stockpiled weaponry. We dismounted
at the rent-a-motorbike shop in Chanía
under the first drops.

At the foot of Lithanon Street, we had a
seedy furnished room just above the harbor.

All that night, the hurricane howled and pounded
against our window.

Through the wall, the *yíayía* complained and bickered
with her mumbling daughter and adolescent
grandson (who looked more like a bull than like a
Minoan gymnast).

All that night, and all through the day that followed,
trapped in bed by roaring expostulations
we made love nine times, and we read, between us,
a thousand pages—

Durrell and Duras brought along from Paris
bookshelves only friendlier when it's raining.
We'd longed for conventual isolation:
here we were close as

we'd get to it, stir-crazy in our two-day
underwear. Pushed out on the street by hunger,
we ate deep-fried pigs' balls in a rank café
behind the market.

In the morning, overcast skies still darkened
Chanía, but the hurricane had abated.
Little knots of fishermen, waiters, clerks from
flooded-out shops stood

near the pier, debating the damage. Old men
swore that fifty years had gone by since they'd seen
such a storm. I think they did, with sparse Greek. We
looked at the water.

Wicker chairs and orange peels bobbed adrift in
slime-green waves that lapped over the retaining

wall to sluice the harborfront shops and bars with
their bloat and sewage.

Dutch and German backpackers trudged outside our
favorite café, waterlogged and scraggly
in among unseasonably shawled basket-
laden town matrons.

Paired monks paced the cruciform aisles inside the
covered market. Up on the hill, the burly
one packed up his saddlebags in the mud-pocked
cobblestone courtyard.

Elysian Fields

"Champs Elysées of Broadway" says the awning
of the café where, every Sunday morning,
young lawyers in old jeans ripped at the knees
do crosswords. Polyglot Lebanese
own it: they've taken on two more shopfronts
and run their banner down all three at once.
Four years ago, their sign, "Au Petit Beurre,"
was so discreet, that, meeting someone there,
I'd tell her the street corner, not the name.
They were in the right place at the right time.
Meanwhile, the poor are trying hard enough.
Outside, on Broadway, people sell their stuff
laid out on blankets, cardboard cartons, towels.
A stout matron with lacquered auburn curls
circles the viridian throw rug
and painted plaster San Martín to hug
a thinner, darker woman, who hugs her
back volubly in Spanish—a neighbor,
I guess, and guess they still have houses.
The man with uncut, browned French paperbacks,
the man with two embroidered gypsy blouses
and three pilled pitiful pairs of plaid slacks
folded beside him on the pavement where
there was a Puerto Rican hardware store
that's been a vacant shopfront for two years
may not. There's a young couple down the block
from our corner: she's tall, gaunt, gangly, Black;
he's short, quick, volatile, unshaven, white.
They set up shop dry mornings around eight.
I've seen him slap her face, jerking her thin
arm like a rag doll's—a dollar kept from him,

she moves too slow, whore, stupid bitch . . . "She's
my wife," he tells a passing man who stops
and watches. If anyone did call the cops
it would be to prevent them and their stacks
of old *Vogues* and outdated science texts
from blocking access to the "upscale bar"
where college boys get bellicose on beer.
"Leave him," would I say? Does she have keys
to an apartment, to a room, a door
to close behind her? What we meant by "poor"
when I was twenty, was a tenement
with clanking pipes and roaches; what we meant
was up six flights of grimed, piss-pungent stairs,
four babies and a baby-faced welfare
worker forbidden to say "birth control."
I was almost her, on the payroll
of New York State Employment Services
—the East 14th Street Branch, whose task it was
to send day workers, mostly Black, to clean
other people's houses. Five-fifteen
and I walked east, walked south, walked up my four
flights. Poor was a neighbor, was next door,
is still a door away. The door is mine.
Outside, the poor work Broadway in the rain.
The cappuccino drinkers watch them pass
under the awning from behind the glass.

One More Car Poem for Julie

I need transmission fluid for the brain.
The sky is a pathetic fallacy.
Even the R-cinq won't start in the rain.

How bad's the Gignac supermarket line
at five-thirty on a wet Saturday?
I need transmission fluid for the brain.

The car, nose upwind of the sodden plain,
grunts like an old sow turning in her sty.
Even the R-cinq won't start in the rain.

"We'll wait. The engine's flooded." You explain
the car's idiosyncracies to me.
I need transmission fluid for the brain.

So do you: both on our own again,
two solitudes stall temporarily.
Even the R-cinq won't start in the rain

and she's a Tour de France-class veteran,
a tough old lady, like we hope to be.
We need transmission fluid for the brain;

she needs to let her gas tank blow-dry, then
roll downhill, nudged by three grizzled *pépés.*
Even the R-cinq won't start in the rain.

Two pounds of coffee, three bottles of wine,
a six-pack, four liters of Perrier . . .
even the R-cinq won't start in the rain:
we need transmission fluid for the brain.

Chiliastic Sapphics

Sunday afternoon at the end of summer:
from the Place des Vosges come a busking harpist's
liquid notes to lap at the traffic noises
outside my window.

Car horns honk: tail end of a Jewish wedding's
automotive crocodile. Bridal party
at the head, they beep toward the *vingtième*, trailing
limp pink tulle streamers.

Flip in a cassette while I read the papers:
drought and famine, massacres. Cloistered sisters'
voices raise the Kyrie. A gay pastor
who was abducted

last week rated photographs and a headline.
This week, men in uniform: an invasion.
Refugees are interviewed crossing borders,
businessmen taken

hostage. An American in a golf cart
mobilizes teenagers to the oilfields.
Crowds in Jordan volunteer for the jihad's
suicide squadrons.

Tanks and aircraft carriers take position
to wage war for Mecca and petrodollars.
Poison gas is brandished. (The Kurds were gassed, and
then, who protested?)

Death to Jews, to infidels, to invaders!
Kill the Arabs! We're going to blast the bastards
off the planet! Journalists feed the slogans
into computers.

They'll be heard tomorrow in every language
(even taking precedence over football).
Holy war or genocide: peace is every-
where untranslated.

Will she be in love with me when I'm fifty?
Will we still have names and our own diseases?
What's become of Pasteur Doucé? His lover
mourns, while reporters

flock toward war. The nuns who attain their limpid
a cappella *O lumière joyeuse*
made their tape four years ago. They'd be singing
it now, at vespers.

At this moment, six o'clock sunlight blazes
roof and cornice opposite, where the neighbors,
just come home from holidays in the country,
throw open windows,

and the price of nectarines and tomatoes
by the kilo was what competing voices
cried in French and Arabic at the market
early this morning.

Annunciation: 8 A.M.

The plaster-dusted forearms of the boys
scaling the next-door building stretch across
my window. Mallets syncopate their noise
to contrapuntal belches of a bus

downstairs. A huge blue wire-and-plastic tent
covers the scaffolding they clamber up.
Here comes a fifty-pound sack of cement
hooked dubiously to a pulley-rope.

They would have looked like angels to Cocteau:
slick brown arms, backs, chests, flecked with fine white powder.
I turn the dial in search of Radio
Classique. It may require something louder

—Tunisian pop?—to neutralize the racket
of what just looks like self-important Men
At Work to me, too close, who will not pack it
in till noon: their job's the civic one.

My job's the monkish notebook on the pine
table facing the window, white-veiled now.
Beside it lies, light-barred in thin sunshine,
an airmail envelope from someone who

once sat across this table, with the pane
of glass behind the sunburst of her hair
reflecting its flat halo on massed rain
clouds above slate roofs I was glad were there

as an excuse to spend the day indoors.
But that was in another incarnation
whose flesh is paper now, not mine, not hers.
Static crackles the chamber-music station;

drills shatter old facades. The day's begun
officially, that started earlier
with gray light, klaxon of a baker's van,
street sweepers' slosh, shards of the dream before

I woke splintering into syllables
nobody, after all, is going to say,
between the horn concerto and the drills,
the morning and the rest of the long day.

Her Ring

Her ring is in a safe-deposit box
with hundred-dollar bills and wills and deeds.
You used to hide my letters with the stock
certificates, unlock a room to read
those night thoughts in a vault under the bank
where we descend this noon: a painless loan
of cash from you to me, for which I thank
you, but tremble. Half as a joke, we sign
a promissory note on a loose-leaf
page: odd, to see your name written with mine.
You fold that, file it in a plastic sleeve,
then rummage in the artifacts to find
and show me what you've just inherited:
your mother's knuckle-duster diamond ring,
a fossil prism in a satin bed.
You model it. I see your hand shaking.
You ask me if I want to try it on
but I won't put that diamond on my hand.
Once, I gave you a ring. You loaned me one.
What I borrowed that day has been returned.

Letter on June 15

I didn't want a crowd. I didn't want
writers' backbiting in a restaurant.
Last night's leftover duck, some chilled Sancerre
(you've called fresh-tasting) beckoned to me more.
I crossed the Pont Sully, into an eight-
forty sunset, toward home, and whom I'd meet.
In the letter that I didn't write,
I tell you, I was meeting you tonight.
You in an envelope; you in the braille
of postmarks footnoting the morning mail.
You, bracketed from life with someone else
though part of every page is what she tells
you; not my morning clarity of bells
to matins, phoned links to life with someone else.
I met you here as if geography
were all that separated you from me,
though hand to hand and lovely mouth to mouth
magnetic north and doubly polar south
are on lost maps, the trails are overgrown.
It's warm, it's almost dark, it's half past ten.
"I can't imagine Paris without you"
was the tearjerker on the radio
when I began to cry in Julie's car
under the Nashville skyline where you were
the bottom line. By the time we got
to Phoenix (with bald tires and gluey hot
seat covers) I was already halfway back
to Paris without you. In time, with luck,
anyone could imagine needing less
than all this food, these books, these clothes: excess
upholstery, distraction, dead wood, bloat.

You're what I had to learn to do without.
I did. But here you are, no farther than
the whirring of the small electric fan
we bought that summer when you had night sweats,
then a sore back, then just a cold, then doubts
that you'd blot out with morning lust against
my chest, my cunt, my mouth, as evidence
that you were present. Later, you'd deny
what you'll admit to now: the late July
three-quarter moon on shuttered bars, the meat
and vegetables, the dim glow when you lit
a candle in the chapel after Mass.
An ancient park attendant clears the grass
of kids who were imagined *jouissance*
when we conceived and miscarried our chance.
We each have whispered, written, other names.
There are more dead for whom to light small flames.
Down on the street, waiters crank up the awning
of the café *en face.* Tomorrow morning
I'll be no farther and no closer than
your walk down to the post office with Jan
along a storm-pocked tertiary road.
Word-children, we will send each other words
that measure distances we have to keep
defining. When I lay me down to sleep
you stack up your day's work sheets on the porch
table, light up, lean back. Two silver birch
trees form a twilit arch above your head.
It's hours before you're going to go to bed.

Quai Saint-Bernard

I take my Sunday exercise riverside,
not quite a local, not quite a transient.
      Dutch houseboats, gravel barges, nose by
      teenagers tanning in day-glo gym shorts.

Waves slick as seal pelts undulate after, like
sun-dappled, ludic, sexual animals
            —if you ignore the floating garbage
            cast by the strollers and weekend sailors.

Three German students nap on their sleeping bags,
backpacks and water bottles niched next to them,
            up on the slope of lawn beside the
            playground, as safe as suburban puppies,

while, underneath a willow, a family:
blonde woman, man like African ebony,
            her mother, almond-golden toddler,
            picnic on Camembert, bread and apples.

I bring my books to sit in my favorite
spot, concrete steps that arc in a half-circle
            out from the water. Sometimes, barges
            pull up and tie up beside my elbow.

Shit! someone's standing inches in back of me,
with all this space . . . From vision's periphery
            I just can make out it's a woman,
            so I relax. Then she walks around me

on down the quai—a derelict madwoman,
drunk, drugged, or tranced, long hair to her knees, with bare
    feet, flowered blouse and filthy trousers,
    teetering there like a tightrope walker.

She pauses, kneels down, flinging her copious
brown, half-soaked hair, a blindfold, in front of her
    so she can't see where she is going
    inches away from the churning water.

Who stops her, leads her farther away from the
edge, even asks her what she was doing there?
    I don't, although she'd come so close her
    serpentine shadow fell on my notebook.

She halts, and sways in front of a sunbathing
young man engrossed in reading a paperback.
    We others watch her staring at him,
    grateful we aren't the one she's chosen.

No crisis: she traverses the half-circle
stone steps, away from water and audience,
    sits in the dust behind a basalt
    statue, lies down like exhausted dogs do.

So I dismiss her, turn back away from her.
So does the almost-naked man opposite.
    We read, relieved of ever knowing
    even what language she might have spoken.

Letter to a Wound

We never had a cabin in the woods.
We never had a yard, a dog, a child.
We never lived in the same neighborhood.
We never ate, half-naked, on a tiled
terrace over the vineyards in Languedoc,
or drank milkshakes on the toweled front seat
of that fifth-hand Chevy pickup truck
whose gears required a clog dance with both feet.
The girl turned round, got older, shut the door
behind her. Twenty-five gone; forty-four
came and went: you're almost thirty; I'm
forty-six. There were other years instead
of all the hours and days we never had.
Mostly, what we never had was time.

Mostly, what we never had was time
to learn the words and pauses each one needed,
look at a known face long enough to read it
right. When we were partners in crime,
we lived in the colloquial sublime:
the getaway jalopy, unimpeded,
swerved toward the exit ramp at breakneck speed. It
wasn't real. What was real? I am stym-
ied by that one, even now. Was I just
a casualty of your twenty-five-
year growing pains? When the cloud of lust
settled on the imaginary drive-
way, you'd left. Not: left room for discussion.
Work it out? I could have been speaking Russian.

Work it out? If I'd been speaking Russian
we couldn't have understood each other less.
"Yes" and "Not this" were different languages.
Here, I've another language, sometimes lush in
an orchard's mouth, sometimes the brisk percussion
of *citadins.* In Iva's outgrown Guess
jeans, by the river, watching barges pass
and gay boys clamber through the underbrush in
cache-sexes, where *bateaux-mouches* perform their deft
swerve, vanishing around l'Ile Saint-Louis,
I think of other years here: with Marie,
alone, with Iva, then with you, alone,
K. J.'s and my first year, alone again.
I think of whom I love, and whom she left.

I think of whom I love, and whom she left.
Years back, when I ragged her about her youth,
she'd tease me that I wasn't old enough
for her. So someone else plunged in that swift
seductive current with youth set adrift.
"You'll like her. She's smart. She's got a kid. She's tough."
(We jaywalked Astor Place.) "I think I'm in love."
"More than you were last time?" I might have laughed.
Tough, smart: I did like her. Smart, tough: she died.
Would it amuse her that a pallbearer
married the widow—or the widower?
(Shades of a British thriller, or a dyke
romance, two kinds of potboiler she liked
to read, with snacks, in bed.) I hope it would.

Two read with snacks in bed. I hoped it would
be like this: daily life I can believe
in, daily. Anyone you love will leave
was what you proved to me the year you did.

So she and I, at first, were closeted
from everyone, ourselves included, grief
not yet, for either (ever) over. We've
made room for grief because it's what we had;
agree the sum of days is all our lives.
One morning, it meant more than being lovers
to walk home with her from the dry cleaner,
our arms heaped up with summer slipcovers.
That night, I was meeting you for dinner.
You wore a torn black ribbon on your sleeve.

You wore a torn black ribbon on your sleeve:
your mother—the mother who adopted
you, not the other one, who left—was dead.
You wore that scrubbed composure the bereaved
wear, after a long dying: drained, relieved.
You, not alone, were going to drive upstate.
"There's a funky French place K. J. and I ate
at, near there—Yvonne's." I wondered if
it would remind you, too, of Fandango
in Paris (where I'd soon be back, solo).
You'd felt safe there, those summer evenings when
we brought a notebook, and shared your good pen.
I wrote a line, you wrote a line, and then
Nadine was there, opened our chilled Meursault.

Nadine was *here,* opened our chilled Meursault
while we wrote vinous couplets. There, Yvonne
broke the cork in half for you and Jan
before she poured your wine, as if she knew.
I know an exigent tall person who
kissed my face in the February sun
that flecked Camille Claudel's bust of Rodin
beneath the gelid trees. It isn't you.

You vetoed one future: don't blur those pasts
that followed the short present you allowed
us. You write, it calmed your mourning that
somebody was right there with you at last
to drive home through the woods beside you—but
we never had a cabin in the woods.

Letter to Julie in a New Decade

I think of you in all that Irish mist
in which you're writing out your solitude
impatiently: the morning's Eucharist
is gruel, or finnan haddie; clouds intrude
on crag and moor and rain-drenched Gothic heap
—at least, they do when I imagine it.
Up on the hills are huddled flocks of sheep
that leave behind them little cairns of shit.
The men tell whoppers and they drink too much.
They all should do something about their teeth.
Has there been anyone you'd like to touch?
Is there a sunset hike across the heath?
It's going to rain again—the sky's like lead.
Mme. Melhing next door is ninety-nine.
I meet her on the street, her daily bread
tucked in an oilcloth shopping bag (no, mine
is string). At least, the woman the Sécu
sends twice a week said she was ninety-eight
last year. (If you live long enough, you get
a Black woman to clean up after you?)
That's only twice a week: five days, she's got
to tend herself. I passed her yesterday
hauling her night-filled plastic chamber pot
to her Turkish-style *WC-sur-palier*.
Across the way, the redhead on the third
floor still chain-smokes shaking out her rugs.
Her mate, in the next window, bends his beard-
ed gray head streetwards while he grooms the dog.
The widow downstairs (I invent that she's
widowed) takes mouthfuls from a red tin cup
she spits out at her ten-foot rubber trees.

A jackhammer was pounding. Now it's stopped
and two Black men in orange worker's pants
take five, light up, and lean against their truck.
Like us, I think, they have two continents,
but not, like us, the luxury and luck
to bridge them, while we can. Another friend
told me, on the phone: her lover found
a lump, is having surgery—happened
in days, two lives completely turned around
toward what could be the end of one, of two
together. She's my father's age, and mine.
I thought of him. I also thought of you,
out with your still-young mother, drinking wine,
one month; the next month, you could only cry
at what one, two, oncologists projected.
We're all dying—but she was going to die
at a velocity no one expected.
My father was forty-six years old
before he "settled down" in a career.
Cancer settled in him. They never told
us what it was. It killed him in a year.
So, *carpe diem:* eat, drink, fuck and write
to glean grace from these chiliastic days?
The left lacks all conviction, and the right—
capitalism with a human face?
If such a beast exists, I haven't met it.
Entrepreneurs and presidents all can
proclaim, then violate the Rights of Man.
As for the rights of woman, oh, forget it.
That's an idea whose day has come, and gone,
they say. Just as an alcoholic tells
herself while tossing back another one:
the "feminist" is always someone else.
A China-doll-faced Polish lesbian

proclaimed, when you say "feminists," we see
housewives in aprons, mules and straggly buns
discussing baby crap and recipes.
A Russian poet, equally *mignonne*
but straight, explained that "feminists," to her,
meant "groups of lesbians," and lesbians
had not formed groups in the USSR.
I heard one on a panel a few nights
ago, read one between two book reviews.
Meanwhile, the Poles rescind abortion rights
and Pamyat opens season on the Jews.
They've got, in Polish, Renée Vivien,
Colette, and *Les Chansons de Bilitis*
—a piquant combination for a *fin
de siècle* in which clitoridectomies
are performed on infants here in France,
posing a quandary for the liberals:
invade the privacy of immigrants
because their custom is to castrate girls?
Sarcasm is too easy when I'm scared
the cocktail party's over, and the feast
of the new century will be prepared
by nationalists, patriarchs and priests.
It's hard to picture fundamentalists
arresting sunbathers and blasting *flics*
while *Blanc Bleu* and *Autour du Monde* persist
in turning bakeries into boutiques
(no *baguettes* in the rue des Francs-Bourgeois,
only *braguettes* on 600-franc jeans)
but jihad followed imam followed shah,
and imams aren't puréed aubergines
(while, in the land that promised that its gold
would be shared work and civil liberties,
big blonde commandoes shoot at twelve-year-olds

and herd them into "camps" for "refugees").
But I was going to write to you, not rant
at you (the code word, we both know, is "shrill"
when some opinionated female won't
address the "universal" or keep still.)
If I live long enough, my small ambition
is, be the next old lady on the third
floor (blessed with indoor plumbing), in condition
to send the next and next-to-the-last word
to you, in some warm green place, with your grown-up
granddaughter, and dogs, where it's not raining.
I hope we won't be jailed, or veiled, or blown up
and have the energy to keep complaining.

For K. J., Between Anniversaries

I'll call you, my time, midday on Saturday.
You're somewhere I can barely imagine you,
      not well, but jauntily describing
      tear gas, no water, no lights, the lizards.

We live like this: I'm often away from you.
Train, airport, car: we synchronize calendars,
      seize what we can, the way we did when
      nobody knew (and we fucked like tomcats).

That was the summer when we were clandestine
nonlovers, stealing passionate mornings till
      lunch break, then more again till nightfall,
      dinner, then over the river, parting.

We left the city I knew I loved before
I knew I loved you: day train to Nice where I
      burned when your body burned against me,
      showed you Provence as it passed the window.

Nights, tousled beds, Cavafian climaxes;
days on the mountains, monks in a Rent-a-Wreck:
      two women of assorted genders
      sharing our bodies like bread, like brandy.

Late August: it was almost by accident
we were together. Nobody knew you were
      with me in Saint-Giraud. The evenings
      lengthened. The cockerels woke us early.

One morning, on our second-hand bicycles
we crossed the vineyards, riding on tractor-paths,
        to go to Mass one village over.
        Showered and brushed in our sun-bleached trousers,

we stood with village women in cardigans
pulled over flowered dresses, and vignerons
        who'd changed out of their sky-blue work clothes,
        singing a hymn we could share: thanksgiving.

Thanksgiving for the passionate friendship we
stopped in a hidden orchard to celebrate,
        then pedaled on to Sunday lunch in
        leaf-dappled light of a village square, where

two mongrels romped in front of the brasserie.
Big, black and furry, bumptiously puppyish,
        they stretched and locked their muzzles in a
        languorous canine embrace that lasted

all through the salad, into the omelette.
When we got up, and back on our bicycles,
        they still were at it, rolling over
        into the shade of the bar together,

heads on each other's flanks by a wine barrel.
Dogs kiss? They mount each other and copulate.
        We liked whatever they were doing,
        grinned as we bicycled slowly homeward.

That evening, we stood under the greengages
which dropped their windfall fruit on our promises,
        lay down again beneath a poplar,
        cradled and lapped by the wine-green valley.

Now, not clandestine, conjugal, workaday,
we're still surprised by partings and meetings when
    lust like a forest fire takes over,
    burning us clean of our expectations.

I wish these lines could end in an orchard where
we stopped and loved each other with generous
    strength, sweating like they do at harvest,
    gasping with joy at the peak, in sunlight.

They end at sunset, back in a room where I've
talked, slept, awakened and lived with you
    where you are with me when you're elsewhere,
    lover and friend, in the ways we've chosen.

An Absent Friend

Perched on a high stool, the auburn sybil
eats Fig Newtons, elbows on the sink,
the other lively hand exhorting. Think
through those words to silences. Think to refill
the teapot. The water's come to a boil.
It's four A.M. Tea steeps. We pour, we drink
it milky, volley talk, talk, link
lines read out loud from some book on the pile
accumulated on the scarred oak table
to some felicity of memory.
The black cat hums like a fridge. The three
daughters are asleep in different rooms.
Through the steamed window on the garden comes
pearl dawnlight, lovely and unremarkable.

Lovely and unremarkable, the clutter
of mugs and books, the almost-empty Fig
Newtons box, thick dishes in a big
tin tray, the knife still standing in the butter,
change like the color of river water
in the delicate shift to day. Thin fog
veils the hedges, where a neighbor dog
makes rounds. "Go to bed. It doesn't matter
about the washing-up. Take this book along."
Whatever it was we said that night is gone,
framed like a photograph nobody took.
Stretched out on a camp cot with the book,
I think that we will talk all night again,
there, or another where, but I am wrong.

Cleis

She's sixteen, and looks like a full-grown woman,
teenaged status hinted at by the acne.
I remember infancy's gold, unblemished
skin. I remember

every time I scolded her, slapped her, wished her
someone whom she wasn't, and let her know it.
Every mother knows she betrays her daughter.
Does she? Maybe.

She was not the builder of model airplanes.
She was not the runner I never could be.
She was not the pillager of my bookshelves,
Rimbaud, or Brontë.

She was not the heroine of a novel.
She was only eight, with a perfect body
caught above the swimming pool, midair, leaping
into blue water

(snapshot: 1982, Vence; she joined me
Air France Unaccompanied Minor). She's the
basic human integer, brown-skinned, golden,
wingless, but flying.

She has breasts and buttocks to keep her earthbound
now. She rereads children's books in her loft bed:
*Little Women, Anne of Green Gables, Robin
Hood,* and *Black Beauty.*

—dreaming herself back out of adolescence
while she talks of cars and her own apartment.
Sixteen is a waiting room: older, younger,
anything's better.

Every day a little bit more a grown-up
face not known yet superimposed on her face
as it turns, a sunflower, out of childhood
"bright and amazing"

like one of her lullabies (by a poet
ragged, old, incontinent, isolated
in a walk-up cluttered with rocks and papers
now; a flamboyant

balladeer, once): cats by the fire in winter,
magic cat-king purring beside the singer,
famine and despair in the cries of scrawny
cats on the pavement.

Years now since I stroked her and sang that to her.
Since her breasts grew, I haven't seen her naked.
Infant sweat's like lavender water; hers is
womanly, pungent.

When I was in love with her, with a lover's
tendency to mythify the beloved,
did I know her better than I do now, when
we know our limits?

Now she is a traveler like the others:
blonde braid, man's hat, jeans and a gray tweed blazer,
pushing one old duffle bag on a trolley,
free, in an airport

full of haggard voyagers, coming, going.
She stops, sees me. Under the sign ARRIVALS
we embrace, and heft the old bag up, one strap
each, on our shoulders.

Dusk: July

Late afternoon rain of a postponed summer:
wet streets, wet slate rooves, swish of tires, wet awnings,
pin-curled neighbor leaning out on her wrought-iron
window guard, smoking,

wet chestnuts, wet lavender by the river's
shades of gray-green. This oversubtle season
will not burst, all clarity, into sunlight.
Petal by petal,

tiger lilies open up in a pitcher,
orange, yellow, stars or beast faces yawning.
Leaves like feast-day offerings round an altar
drop on the carpet.

I would love my love, but my love is elsewhere.
I would take a walk with her in the evening's
milky pearl. I'd sleep with my arms around her
confident body,

arms and legs asprawl like an adolescent.
We're not adolescents. Our friends are dying
and between us nothing at all is settled
except our loving.

We've loved other bodies the years have altered:
knuckles swollen, skin slackened, eyelids grainy;
bodies that have gone back to earth, the synapse
of conscience broken.

Softly, softly, speak of it, but say something.
We are middle-aged and our friends are dying.
What do we lie down beside when we lie down
alone, together?

If I could remember the names, the places,
rooms and faces, gestures and conversations,
I'd have some excuse for the years passed through me
like air, like water:

school friends who turned into suburban matrons;
bar friends, one-night stands, who are dead of AIDS, or
tenured, or in jail, or suburban matrons;
great-aunts, grandparents

of whom I had nothing to tell my daughter.
Those dead Jews on both sides of the Atlantic
disappear again as the year two thousand
washes us under.

Seize the days, the days, or the years will seize them,
leaving just the blink of a burnt-out lightbulb
with a shard of filament left inside that
ticks when it's shaken.

Fix the days in words and the years will seize them
anyway: a bracket of dates, an out-of-
print book, story nobody told, rooms locked and
phone disconnected,

cemetery no one will ever visit.
Who knows where my grandparents' graves are? Who cut
through the gauze unveiling my mother's tombstone?
I don't. I didn't.

Light is still alive in the table lamp I
switch on in the nine o'clock twilight; music
still alive in street noise; mine one more shadow
drawing the curtains.

I just want to wake up beside my love who
wakes beside me. One of us will die sooner;
one of us is going to outlive the other,
but we're alive now.

For a Fiftieth Anniversary

The King of Denmark wore a yellow star.
French Jews paid for their own with one textile
ration point: not what pétainists wore
—and the jew squats on the window sill . . .

One thought it blasphemy his girls learn Torah.
One was the great-uncle of Simone Weil.
One was deported and so was the other
—and the jew squats on the window sill . . .

Habit and ideology illumine
banal perceptions of the human world.
The next-door neighbor's something less than human
—and the jew squats on the window sill . . .

The Eastern intellectual elite,
the ACLU-carded liberal,
the ecologists and the effete
and the jew squat on the window sill

—or Palestinian, Croat or Greek:
invest with otherness, isolate, kill
the Paki or the nigger or the spic
—and the jew squats on the window sill . . .

Seventeen then, she's sixty-six, alive
this year to give her testimonial:
"Two days after the Fête de la Bastille,
I mean, two days from when it would have been,
another year, before the occupation,
I watched my mother and my brother leave

—the orders said "all children under sixteen"
and "no unnecessary conversation"—
on what had been a city bus until
they gave it a new route, to the Vel d'Hiv.
I didn't see either one of them again."
—and the jew squats on the window sill . . .

Street Scenes I

Wool scarf and leather
jacket weather on the rue de Turenne
this June, any June.

Rain again, or just
a fine film of construction workers' dust
from the new posh shop-

front being installed
downstairs, or the roofers across the street?
Dust. Tentative sun

cheers the freshly scaled
facade, then a cloud passes, and it fades.
Three Algerian

men in blue denim
wait for the bus, while a slim Black woman
with a red briefcase

shelters in the door-
way of the upscale children's clothing store,
not dressed for the wind.

The Home Visitor
from the Sécu knocks politely next door,
politely's let in,

The names of clouds are
more relevant than the names of flowers.
Wind-tattered roses

lean over the stairs
going down to the Quai Saint-Bernard, where
it's too cold to go,

but the young couple
opposite have a window box: yellow
and purple pansies.

Now the rain. Thunder,
a real storm—will my salmon begonia
breathe, or be battered?

Street Scenes II

After lunch, the Sunday strollers boil
on the pavement, two miles from Belleville,
which may be the upcoming *quartier*
now that fashion's priced out the Marais.
Stretch-silk jeans, antiqued American
patchwork quilts (hand-sewn, but in Taiwan)
rag-doll Black girls and rag-doll Uncle Sams
are sold in what still was the Hammam
Saint-Paul last year. There, Jewish matrons, girt
with goosefat, had their nails done, had dessert
and some discreet attention to their hair,
had tea and time to gossip in lounge chairs
on steaming tiles beside the pool, or nap.
There, granddaughters and foreigners swam laps,
sweated, were flogged with twigs, were rubbed and rolled
over, kneaded and pummeled, doused with cold
water, to join them, panting, on the tiles,
or risk the verdict of the eight-foot scales.
The Jewish matrons were Tunisian
Jews. The French Jews mostly disappeared
in forty-two: the Vélodrome d'Hiver,
Beaune-la-Rolande, Drancy—then the trains.
Their street is being frosted to a myth.
The cowboy-boot boutique rubs doorsills with
a new shop selling Yemenite cassettes
and hand-painted Israeli seder plates.
Ben-Simon the butcher coexists
with an architectural palimpsest
of doors and windows: heavy oak and brass
four hundred years old, filigree and glass
of the last *fin de siècle*, fresh concrete

pavement of this one, widening the street
so international pedestrians
can loiter. Redispersed Jews seeking roots,
they price the impossible purple snakeskin boots
and queue for lunch at the falafel stands
with sallow cousins in ageless black coats.

Street Scenes III

Dusted with flour, pine-gold, the wand of bread
protrudes from a fruit-knobbed plastic Monoprix
shopping bag, balances gallantly
on a bike basket, is tucked under a red
cardigan sleeve, blue coverall sleeve, fine gray
flannel sleeve. Everyone carries it:
acolyte's candle, torch of the athlete,
common denominator.
                    From what bakery
on the morning of the seventeenth of July,
his arms piled with baguettes, did the young man come
to one locked gate of the Vélodrome d'Hiver?
French guards tore up the loaves they took from him
and flung them at the thousands—Jews—penned there
—children, women and men—on their way to die.

Street Scenes IV

Seven-thirty and lightly the rain continues.
Yes I am one of them and also I am not
one of them: late shoppers buying what they forgot
in the morning, tired workers jostling from various venues,
kids on the loose to loaf. Waiters place menus
on outdoor tables they've just optimistically set.
The Germans eat early, the younger British eat late,
but not outdoors in the rain. Umbrellas in use
joust on the narrow sidewalk: the shoppers pass
the workers pass the tourists pass the waiters
stay put. I am a shopper going home
which is where I've come from work, which is where I'll later
wait on myself. I'm a stranger who'll be some-
where else when the satcheled children file back to class.

Street Scenes V

The German tour bus
pulls out of the sleepy street.
No one is sorry.

After group dinner
they sang group songs in German
under our windows.

Neighbors remember
songs in the street like that in
nineteen forty-one.

They're European
brothers and sisters now, but
they pull their curtains.

Two streets over, some
neighbors didn't come back from
the Vel d'Hiv, Drancy.

They were babies in
forty-one, or not born, those
charter-bus singers.

There were babies be-
hind barbed wire at Drancy. When
should they have been born?

Days of 1992

"Pray for the souls of the antisemites."
— Alfred Corn, "Somerset Alcaics"

I spent the morning waxing the furniture,
thick orange beeswax sprayed on a chamois cloth,
        dull glow on what was flat and dusty,
        odor of beeswax, a tinge of honey.

Storm-crumbled plaster, storm-swollen window frames
work for the bookish Orthodox carpenter;
        then a discussion with the plumber
        who will dismantle the bathtub Thursday.

Low, heavy clouds, unbroken humidity
(like Great Lakes Gray in darkest America)
        makes indoors smell like dirty linen.
        Open the windows! Invite the breeze in!

If it were Sunday, I'd do my market run
Boulevard Richard Lenoir: half past nine I'd
        be filling up my wicker basket,
        bathed in the polyglot cries of vendors.

Chard, onions, eggplant, cherries and strawberries,
ecru *pleurotes*, their undersides filigreed
        to be sautéed with breast of chicken?
        Trout? Or a skate wing (black butter, capers).

But it's not Sunday, only a workaday
Tuesday, after the bleak anniversary:

my chosen people gave my people
up to the brownshirted blond invaders.

One generation, now, since the war stories,
since the betrayals, since the internment camps,
    since the haggard few survivors
    got off the trains that had damned, then saved them,

just to confront revisionist bureaucrats.
As I live out my chosen diaspora
    watching the clouds and writing letters,
    what earthly good is my faceless mourning?

I went for a massage in rue Rambuteau
from a wiry, bearded Jew in his sixties
    born two streets over from his office.
    He and his parents endured the war years

hiding out in a village in Perigord.
More lucky than two-thirds of their relatives,
    they never saw a single German.
    "If we'd stayed here, I would not be here now."

What did my neighbors do when the gendarmes came
Jew-hunting in this Jewish arrondissement?
    I've never asked my next-door neighbor:
    frail centenarian who was fifty-

two then, a few years older than I am, now.
I'm frightened to investigate memories:
    maybe she liked Pétain, perhaps she
    told the gendarmes where a man was hiding,

maybe she knew no Jews, ignored the buses,
maybe she hid a scared Jewish girl in her

dank Turkish toilet on the landing
until an aunt with forged papers fetched her.

So I invent her, paint her with politics
past, while she follows soaps on her TV set,
        cleans, totes her bread and wine upstairs, feeds
        sparrows in the Place des Vosges dry bread crumbs,

reads daily papers, rightish and populist.
I wait to hear the Sécu come check on her
        mornings. She's background music to my
        life for eight years here: how much longer?

She goes, and I go, into our histories
as the century's flame-darkened ending
        silences us if we've stayed silent,
        letting the cries of the street subsume us.

CANCER WINTER

Year's End

for *Audre Lorde and Sonny Wainwright*

Twice in my quickly disappearing forties
someone called while someone I loved and I were
making love to tell me another woman
had died of cancer.

Seven years apart, and two different lovers:
underneath the numbers, how lives are braided,
how those women's deaths and lives, lived and died, were
interleaved also.

Does lip touch on lip a memento mori?
Does the blood-thrust nipple against its eager
mate recall, through lust, a breast's transformations
sometimes are lethal?

Now or later, what's the enormous difference?
If one day is good, is a day sufficient?
Is it fear of death with which I'm so eager
to live my life out

now and in its possible permutations
with the one I love? (Only four days later,
she was on a plane headed west across the
Atlantic, work-bound.)

Men and women, mortally wounded where we
love and nourish, dying at thirty, forty,
fifty, not on barricades, but in beds of
unfulfilled promise:

tell me, senators, what you call abnormal?
Each day's obits read as if there's a war on.
Fifty-eight-year-old poet dead of cancer:
warrior woman

laid down with the other warrior women.
Both times when the telephone rang, I answered,
wanting not to, knowing I had to answer,
go from two bodies'

infinite approach to a crest of pleasure
through the disembodied voice from a distance
saying one loved body was clay, one wave of
mind burst and broken.

Each time we went back to each other's hands and
mouths as to a requiem where the chorus
sings death with irrelevant and amazing
bodily music.

Cancer Winter

for Rafael Campo and Hayden Carruth

Syllables shaped around the darkening day's
contours. Next to armchairs, on desks, lamps
were switched on. Tires hissed softly on the damp
tar. In my room, a flute concerto played.
Slate roofs glistened in the rain's thin glaze.
I peered out from a cave like a warm bear.
Halls lights flicked on as someone climbed the stairs
across the street, blinked out: a key, a phrase
turned in a lock, and something flew open.
I watched a young man at his window write
at a plank table, one pooled halogen
light on his book, dim shelves behind him, night
falling fraternal on the flux between
the odd and even numbers of the street.

I woke up, and the surgeon said, "You're cured."
Strapped to the gurney, in the cotton gown
and pants I was wearing when they slid me down
onto the table, made new straps secure
while I stared at the hydra-headed O.R.
lamp, I took in the tall, confident, brown-
skinned man, and the ache I couldn't quite call pain
from where my right breast wasn't anymore
to my armpit. A not-yet-talking head,
I bit dry lips. What else could he have said?
And then my love was there in a hospital coat;
then my old love, still young and very scared.
Then I, alone, graphed clock hands' asymptote
to noon, when I would be wheeled back upstairs.

The odd and even numbers of the street
I live on are four thousand miles away
from an Ohio February day
snow-blanketed, roads iced over, with sleet
expected later, where I'm incomplete
as my abbreviated chest. I weigh
less—one breast less—since the Paris-gray
December evening, when a neighbor's feet
coming up ancient stairs, the feet I counted
on paper were the company I craved.
My calm right breast seethed with a grasping tumor.
The certainty of my returns amounted
to nothing. After terror, being brave
became another form of gallows humor.

At noon, an orderly wheeled me upstairs
via an elevator hung with Season's
Greetings streamers, bright and false as treason.
The single room the surgeon let us share
the night before the knife was scrubbed and bare
except for blush-pink roses in a vase on
the dresser. Veering through a morphine haze on
the cranked bed, I was avidly aware
of my own breathing, my thirst, that it was over—
the week that ended on this New Year's Eve.
A known hand held, while I sipped, icewater,
afloat between ache, sleep, lover and lover.
The one who stayed would stay; the one would leave.
The hand that held the cup next was my daughter's.

It's become a form of gallows humor
to reread the elegies I wrote
at that pine table, with their undernote
of cancer as death's leitmotiv, enumer-
ating my dead, the unknown dead, the rumor
of random and pandemic deaths. I thought
I was a witness, a survivor, caught
in a maelstrom and brought forth, who knew more
of pain than some, but learned it loving others.
I need to find another metaphor
while I eat up stories of people's mothers
who had mastectomies. "She's eighty-four
this year, and *fine*!" Cell-shocked, I brace to do
what I can, an unimportant exiled Jew.

The hand that held the cup next was my daughter's
—who would be holding shirts for me to wear,
sleeve out, for my bum arm. She'd wash my hair
(not falling yet), strew teenager's disorder
in the kitchen, help me out of the bathwater.
A dozen times, she looked at the long scar
studded with staples, where I'd suckled her,
and didn't turn. She took me / I brought her
to the surgeon's office, where she'd hold
my hand, while his sure hand, with its neat tool, snipped
the steel, as on a revised manuscript
radically rewritten since my star
turn nursing her without a "nursing bra"
from small, firm breasts, a twenty-five-year-old's.

I'm still alive, an unimportant Jew
who lives in exile, voluntarily
or not: Ohio's alien to me.
Death follows me home here, but I pay dues
to stay alive. White cell count under two:
a week's delay in chemotherapy
stretches it out: Ohio till July?
The Nazarenes and Pentecostals who
think drinking wine's a mortal sin would pray
for me to heal, find Jesus, go straight, leave.
But I'm alive, and can believe I'll stay
alive a while. Insomniac with terror,
I tell myself, it isn't the worst horror.
It's not Auschwitz. It's not the Vel d'Hiv.

I had "breasts like a twenty-five-year-old,"
and that was why, although a mammogram
was done the day of my year-end exam
in which the doctor found the lump, it told
her nothing: small, firm, dense breasts have and hold
their dirty secrets till their secrets damn
them. Out of the operating room
the tumor was delivered, sectioned, cold-
packed, pickled, to demonstrate to residents
an infiltrative ductal carcinoma
(with others of its kind). I've one small, dense
firm breast left, and cell-killer pills so no more
killer cells grow, no eggs drop. To survive
my body stops dreaming it's twenty-five.

It's not Auschwitz. It's not the Vel d'Hiv.
It's not gang rape in Bosnia or
gang rape and gutting in El Salvador.
My self-betraying body needs to grieve
at how hatreds metastasize. Reprieved
(if I am), what am I living for?
Cancer, gratuitous as a massacre,
answers to nothing, tempts me to retrieve
the white-eyed panic in the mortal night,
my father's silent death at forty-eight,
each numbered, shaved, emaciated Jew
I might have been. They wore the blunt tattoo,
a scar, if they survived, oceans away.
Should I tattoo my scar? What would it say?

No body stops dreaming it's twenty-five,
or twelve, or ten, when what is possible's
a long road poplars curtain against loss, able
to swim the river, hike the culvert, drive
through the open portal, find the gold hive
dripping with liquid sweetness. Risible
fantasy, if, all the while, invisible
entropies block the roads, so you arrive
outside a ruin, where trees bald with blight
wane by a river drained to sluggish mud.
The setting sun looks terribly like blood.
The hovering swarm has nothing to forgive.
Your voice petitions the indifferent night:
"I don't know how to die yet. Let me live."

Should I tattoo my scar? What would it say?
It could say "K. J.'s Truck Stop" in plain Eng-
lish, highlighted with a nipple ring
(the French version: Chez K. J. / Les Routiers).
I won't be wearing falsies, and one day
I'll bake my chest again at Juan-les-Pins,
round side and flat, gynandre/androgyne,
close by my love's warm flanks (though she's sun-shy
as I should be: it's a carcinogen
like smoked fish, caffeine, butterfat and wine).
O let me have my life and live it too!
She kissed my breasts, and now one breast she kissed
is dead meat, with its pickled blight on view.
She'll kiss the scar, and then the living breast.

I don't know how to die yet. Let me live!
Did Etty Hillesum think that, or Anne Frank,
or the forty-year-old schoolteacher the bank
robber took hostage when the cop guns swiv-
eled on them both, or the seropositive
nurse's aide, who, one long-gone payday, drank
too much, fucked whom? or the bag lady who stank
more than I wished as I came closer to give
my meager change? I say it, bargaining
with the *contras* in my blood, immune
system bombarded but on guard. Who's gone?
The bookseller who died at thirty-nine,
poet, at fifty-eight, friend, fifty-one,
friend, fifty-five. These numbers do not sing.

She'll kiss the scar, and then the living breast,
and then, again, from ribs to pit, the scar,
but only after I've flown back to her
out of the unforgiving Middle West
where my life's strange, and flat disinterest
greets strangers. At Les-Saintes-Maries-de-la-Mer,
lust pulsed between us, pulsed in the plum grove where
figs dropped to us like manna to the blessed.
O blight that ate my breast like worms in fruit,
be banished by the daily pesticide
that I ingest. Let me live to praise
her breathing body in my arms, our wide-
branched perennial love, from whose taproot
syllables shape around the lengthening days.

Friends, you died young. These numbers do not sing
your requiems, your elegies, our war
cry: at last, not "Why me?" but "No more
one-in-nine, one-in-three, rogue cells killing
women." You're my companions, traveling
from work to home to the home I left for
work, and the plague, and the poison which might cure.
The late sunlight, the morning rain, will bring
me back to where I started, whole, alone,
with fragrant coffee into which I've poured
steamed milk, book open on the scarred pine table.
I almost forget how close to the bone
my chest's right side is. Unremarkable,
I woke up, still alive. Does that mean "cured"?

August Journal

How does it feel, in this ephemeral flesh,
to be back at my work table, to sit
looking out the window while a flush
of late sun brightens scrubbed stone opposite,
illuminates known neighbors' unknown rooms,
just as it shone a year, two years ago
when I, immortal as an eight-year-old,
looked out in my clean, unscarred, unbroken skin
(the oily selfhood I'm sequestered in,
the body I'm not going to leave alive,
whose guard—I didn't know it yet—was down)?
If I'm one of the victims, who survives?
If I'm—reach for it—a survivor, who
are the victims? The heroic dead,
the ones who died in despair, the ones who died
in terror, the exhausted ones who died
tired? I'm tired of terror and despair
and having to be brave. I want the dull
workdays and nights of unexceptional
unmarked life, with eyelashes and hair.
It *is* exceptional to die in bed
at ninety-eight, not having been gassed, shot,
wrung dry with dysentery, drowned at birth
in a basin for unwanted girls.
The unexceptional beg on the street
outside Red Apple, outside Monoprix
(he's young, Black, AIDS-thin, with a brindled cat;
she's dark-haired, white, butch, with a Labrador),
Back in Paris, she's there; back in New York
he's there: if one's gone, when will I know it?
For themselves, they will not disappear:

they'll endure whatever they endure,
two years outside a supermarket door
not being sufficient. Life (and death) hold more
bad cards in store than that, bad cards in store
for the complacent housewives walking by:
the mammogram, the colonoscopy.

The sun seeps in through windows I remember.
Now the young couple on the third-floor-left
have a baby (sometime since December)
and crocheted curtains in the front-room window.
Across the hall from them, the little widow
was away (her rubber tree went sallow,
went brown) but now she's back, and leaning out
to watch the menswear wholesaler's young, stout
Arab apprentice load a truck with suits.
Behind me: silence, an occupied
cold-water flat. Madame Mehling has died
at one hundred and two, exceptional
and humdrum as the sparrows that she fed
on fine days, the last night's leftover bread
through two world wars till now. In the damp hall
downstairs, atop the green recycling bin
were piled small, threadbare jacket, dresses, shoes,
aprons, sexagenarian saucepans.
The century of life she had to lose
is lost, the century of memory
evaporated, a scent in the air,
a light, halt step I won't hear on the stairs.
Her fiancé died in the First World War;
she worked four decades in a creamery.
Was it one hundred years of solitude
or of spinsterly sociability
with cronies all around the neighborhood?

Rapid, high-pitched exchanges while TV
noise blared were frequent in the afternoons
as I came up the stairs, thinking that soon
I'd spend an afternoon talking with her.

A century of memory: I talk
as if I could remember: was that walk
along the beach in Normandy before
or after lunch—four days ago! (The war
forty-nine years past, cathedral towers
patched up, museum garden clocked with flowers.)
Carved stones from hen yards, as if magnetized,
pile in the cloister from which they'd been prised
by mercenaries when Napoleon
undid what Jacobins had not undone:
the past—priest-ridden, hunger-blighted, king-
despoiled sump heap where wit, inquiry, reason
flourished for an enigmatic season.
A hundred years before Madame Mehling
was born in some dim suburb, then still green;
a hundred years before my Austrian
Jewish grandparents, both aged sixteen,
fled one more pogrom, as far as London,
the season turned (as it would turn, again):
the flaming summer of a violent spring
promised a raising and a leveling,
with Jews and women hailed as "Citizen."

And turned again, as it will turn toward fall
where I sit, tethered to a present tense
whose intimations of mortality
may ultimately make no difference
to anyone, except of course to me,
and finally, to nobody at all

(a touch of solipsism worthy of
an acned seventeen-year-old in love).
My life is wider than these windowpanes:
one best-beloved friend, beloved friends
in towns and cities on two continents,
some of whom couldn't pronounce each other's names.
Upon my body is superimposed
the map of a Europe I never knew:
my olive skin, my eyes, my hips, my nose
all mark me as an Ashkenazi Jew
if anyone were looking for a mark
to indicate the designated prey.
I'm more the Jew pursued into the dark
than the scrubbed Yank marching through Normandy.
After our songs became ash on the tongue,
after our tongues were ash, after we took
our leave of being old and being young,
can any Jew stay indoors with a book
and ruminate upon her own disease,
present or past, absorbed, alone, aloof?
I could have been one of the children seized
that day at 22, rue des Ecouffes.
I could have been one of the two-year-olds
not knowing quite how to pronounce my name
penned in a littered courtyard, blotched with cold
behind barbed wire, until the transports came
to what is now a suburb on the way
to the airport, utterly banal,
whose name unflinching bus drivers will say.
Some other names: Touvier, Bousquet, Laval.
I know those names, but not the children's names
"deported to the East" in cattle cars.
Can any Jew praise life and fail to claim
a share for them of bread, of books, of stars?
As if they didn't have enough of stars

and uninflected gray or black or blue
skies glimpsed through grilled gaps from the cattle cars,
stars, skies, they starved and froze and died below.
Later, the patriotic hordes of France
shaved and tarred and whipped the women whose
neighbors said, they slept with the occupants:
not the police who rounded up the Jews;
not the officials who determined "race";
not the French guards of French internment camps
who hurried their dazed charges up the ramps
into the death trains: passed without a trace
to middle age, old age, to death in bed
(exceptional) perhaps, at ninety-eight,
perhaps having forgotten what they did
without much thought, much mercy, or much hate.
O Europe of old stairways and dead Jews!
But every Saturday at half past noon
black-bearded fathers, pale, dark-suited sons,
daughters in frills and patent-leather shoes
walk home toward lunch from Sabbath services.
(Where are the mothers? They don't have to cook
on Shabbes!) Stubborn people of the Book,
renewed after such disappearances,
though you are not my past, you are my past
(there are no atheists in a pogrom).
My future, though, is coming toward me fast
from elsewhere, and I cannot know where from
—the night-without-a-morning of disease,
the afternoon of long, exceptional
life as summer modulates to fall,
the flame-erupted dusk of history?
All I can know is the expanding moment,
present, infinitesimal, infinite,
in which the late sun enters without comment
eight different sets of windows opposite.

DATE DUE		
JUL - 3 1995		
JUL 2 3 2001		
	WITHDRAWN	